WHEN
SILENCE
BLOOMS

COLLECTION OF POETRY

fragments of a journey- from heartbreak to healing, from silence to voice...

SASIKALA ALAPPAT

ink Scribe

ink

When Silence Blooms

Publisher: Inkscribe Media Pvt. Ltd

ISBN Number: 978-1-966421-69-6

"I got the most beautiful me in the journey
from you to me…"

To the beloved soul who lifted me from the ashes of my past lives into the light of becoming

Contents

.

Prologue

Life is a beautiful, yet painful journey. Along the way—whether it's long or short—we cross paths with many people. Some places, some faces, and certain moments stay etched in our memories forever.

When we share a deep connection with someone or something, it stirs a kind of restlessness. Out of that restlessness, poetry is born. All of my poems are close to my soul. That doesn't mean I consider myself a great writer—far from it. For me, poetry is a medicine for my aching soul. Often, I find that words fail to fully express what I truly feel.

Many of these poems were originally written in Malayalam, my mother tongue. Translating them into English was not easy, and I know there may be imperfections. I used to blog regularly in Malayalam during its early days, but somewhere along the way, the writing paused.

Over time, I've been lucky to connect with a few kindred souls—people who truly understood my words. Their warmth, encouragement, and faith in me led to this collection. Without them, this may have stayed hidden in my notebooks and forgotten folders.

I know I've only written a drop from the ocean of feelings within me. But perhaps this is the beginning—of letting the words flow again, even when they slip from my pen.

Yours,

Sasikala Alappat

Of Love and Longing

Between You and Me

Between you and me,
dreams are born—
countless as the stars
that scatter themselves
across the night sky.

Between you and me,
a sigh flows like the tide—
waves aching
to kiss the shore,
yet pulled away
by the cruel hands of fate.

Between you and me,
time runs—
elusive,
laughing at our grasp,
as though it tricked us
into believing
we had control.

Between you and me,
memories gleam—
pearls strung
from moments once shared,
a garland
we wove together
in the quiet hush
of love's beginning.

How can we forget
even for a moment—
when an undying river
flows between us,
carrying the echo
of every word
we never stopped saying?

How can dreams fade
when the fire of love
still burns
quietly,
fiercely,
between us?

How can the night complain
of this silence—
when the hush we share
is not emptiness,
but a kiss
only silence can give?

And how can time speak
of sorrow,
or name this
depression,
when the smile on my lips
still holds
the soft trace
of your kiss?

Still I Cannot Shift from Being You

Still,
I cannot shift
from being you.

You opened a world—
woven in love
and fragile fantasies—
then flew
somewhere beyond my reach.

And I…
was left
trapped in that magic,
a butterfly
caught in your absence,
wings trembling,
breathless,
broken.

Now, I see—
those words,
"I am with you,"
were only dreams
I whispered to myself.

I cannot cry.
And I cannot
unlove you.

The fault is mine.
Mine alone.

Mine—
for daring to dream
again,
in this weary,
hopeless life.

Mine—
for watering dead roots
with the rain of my love,
believing
they could bloom once more.

Mine—
for kissing
wilted sunflower petals
back to life,

for letting them drink
sunlight
they were never meant to feel again.

Yes,
I know.
The fault is mine.

But even now—
even in the silence
and the ruin—
I cannot
shift
from being
you.

Love and Friendship

God appeared before me
in the stillness
of a deep, forgotten dream.

A gentle voice echoed—
"Do you want love,
or friendship?"

The question hung in the air,
sudden,
unsettling.

Yet without doubt,
I chose love—
because my heart
had already chosen you.

You leaned close,
your breath like a secret breeze—
"I am always with you,"
you whispered into my ear.

And I bloomed—
like a flower touched
by its first sunlight.

Spring came,
spilling colors
into the corners
of our lives.

Your heartbeat
became a melody
only I could hear.

But then—
a flicker,
a moment,
a flash—

And you vanished
from my dream.

In your place,
God returned—
smiling gently,
almost knowingly.

"Love is momentary,"
God said.
"Friendship is forever."

Then, like a breeze
through open windows,
God was gone.

Now,
I wait still—
in the hush between sleep and morning,
for God to return
just once more,

so I can ask—
not for love this time,
but for the gift
of your never-ending
friendship.

The Place

The place
where words
go to die.

Where 'you' and 'I'
once dissolved
into "we."

The place
where souls
that were once whole,
once one,
find each other again—
without beginning,
without end.

A place
where goodbyes
are never spoken,
where parting
is a wound
no heart
can bear.

The place
where the ache
of separation
bleeds quietly
through time,
and memory
holds us
like a trembling breath.

The place
where words
fall silent—
because silence
knows us better.

The place
where we are reborn—
not as strangers,
but as echoes
of the same flame.

The Journey

You came to me
like a shadow—
soft and sudden—
when I was walking
along the edges
of death.

Never in my life
had I desired anything
as deeply
as I desired you.
And so,
I held your hand—
with wonder,
with trembling joy.

When I discovered
that my dreams
were yours too,
I felt a light
rise within me,
pure
and complete.

We grew weary,
sometimes—
under the heat
of our past lives,
the scorch
of what we once carried.
We stepped back,
knowing
our paths
were not the same.

Yet now and then,
your shadow
gently covered my eyes
from behind—
and stars
would shimmer again
in the sky
of our shared hope.

Even the cactus
of separation
could not stop
the rose of love
from blooming
between us.

When I stumbled,
dragging the baggage
of memory,
you led me forward—
like the sun
guiding
a sunflower's gaze.

I wonder sometimes:
do your feet
tremble
beneath you?
Or is it the echo
of some distant call
that slows
your steps?

Still,
you walk ahead,
and sigh behind—
and in quiet moments,
you reach for my hand.

And so,
together,
we continue
this journey.

The Distance I Cannot Keep

As usual,
I walked out of you
before sleep took me—
leaving behind
villages,
cities,
hills,
rivers,
and seas.

I vowed
never to return.
Promised myself
I wouldn't trap you
in the helpless knots
of my love.

I imagined you
alone,
seated beneath
a tree
bare of words,
where even silence
refused to bloom.

I kept walking—
leaving behind
everything
that reminded me
of you.

Villages.
Cities.
Hills.
Rivers.
Seas.

But then—
as always—
morning came.

And I woke
clinging
closer to you
than ever before,
my heart pressed
against your chest,
as if
even in my dreams,
I could not bear
the distance
I had promised
to keep.

Realization

I was tired—
frozen—
when I realized
you were only a dream:
a tender touch on my wounds,
a fleeting smile,
a star
in my darkened sky.

But I rose—
reborn—
the moment I understood:
to fly,
I must first tend to my wounds,
gently dress them with courage,
and plant seeds of hope
deep in the hollow of my heart.

I must grow my own wings again—
stronger,
wider,
mine.

And in that journey—
from you
to me—
I met
the most beautiful
version
of myself.

Who Are You to Me?

Who are you to me?
Why do I feel I am you, whenever you're beside me?

Though we never sat for hours, gazing into each
other's eyes,
why do I see myself in the depths of yours?

You never spoke of hope—
not even a word—
yet when you're near,
it feels as if your soul quietly embraces mine.

You never hurt me,
not even once.
Still, when you're far away,
I feel a sorrow too deep for words.

I am puzzled—
searching for the meaning of your song...

And when my heart whispers
that I may not dwell in your thoughts,
you return to me like a breath of relief.

It feels as though
you and I were shaped
from the same clay,
by the same divine hand.

There's a wholeness in me
only present when you are near—
a longing to remain
forever in your presence.

The 'me' in you,
that I never knew existed...

And yet,
we move through life
as though we are strangers,
as though we never knew.

Still, I gaze forward,
wondering how time will draw our fates together.

You drift away—
like a Sufi
in search of life's deeper meaning.

And your shadow lingers,
etched into my eyes,
even as darkness swallows the light.

Have You Ever Waited?

Have you ever waited
for a word
from the one you love most?

Not a letter,
not a whisper,
just one word
to cross the silence
and find you.

The minutes stretch,
become hours,
then days—
until time itself
feels like a cruel companion.

Sometimes,
the clock grows wings
and rushes ahead,
mocking your stillness.
Other times,
the night pierces you—
its silence sharp
as nails.

Dawn arrives
without warning,
without speaking.
Sunlight slips
through the cracks of memory,
falling softly
on the ache you carry.
It makes your tears
glow
like morning dew
on broken dreams.

Have you ever waited
for a word
from the one
who once made silence sweet?

The sky darkens—
clouds of despair
gather quietly,
tightening around your breath.

Thoughts crackle
like lightning—
sharp, sudden,
uninvited.

And then the rain comes.
Not from the sky,
but from the soul.
It pours down,
carrying the weight
of all that was unspoken,
all that was meant
but never said.

Have you ever waited
for a word
that never came?

All Roads Still Lead to You

Some moments,
I drift back
into the past—
and wonder
how I survived
those storm-heavy days.

How did I ever find
a shore
to anchor my broken self?

Back then...
I could barely breathe,
choking on the poison
seeping
from the polished shells
of a love
that had ensnared me.

It was then I learned—
hell is not elsewhere;
hell blooms quietly
on this very earth.

I searched
for peace
in the shadow of death,
whispered to the silence
for a way out.

But a few beloved faces
stood
like trembling lights—
their futures
fragile,
tied to mine.
If I disappeared,
they might dissolve
into hunger.

So I stayed.

And now,
today...
I see it differently.

The thorns once hurled
onto my path
were only
flowers in disguise.

The blood that spilled
from my feet
were not wounds—
they were red pearls,
marking each step
I took
in the name of love.

The cries that tore
from my soul
were never screams.
They were lyrics—
fragments
of the song
that was always ours.

And still—
still—
every road I walk
turns
softly,
inevitably,
toward you.

Rebirth and Separation

Rebirth

Do you believe
in rebirth?

Not now.
But once,
I did.

Once,
I yearned
to find you again
in another life—
to reach for you
without shame,
without begging
for love.

But not anymore.

Let me not wander
behind you
like a ghost
with open hands.

Let this lifeless wood
not echo
with the broken music
of my desire.

Let my dreams
not burn
in the fire
of this chest—
where longing
and despair
lie tangled.

Let the love
that once flowed
from your eyes
never find its way
to my pen again,
turning grief
into poetry.

Let time
not laugh
as it tosses me
from you—
again and again,
like a cruel tide.

.

Let even
our shadows
refuse
to meet—
even across
the great distances.

How many times
have I already died
in this life?

Now,
I am ready—
to die
once more.

But this time,
without a rebirth…

As Usual

As usual,
you sat near me
when tears rolled down my cheeks.

You said nothing—
and neither did I.
Yet somehow,
it felt
as if we had spoken.

You didn't lean on my chest,
but still—
my heart tilted
toward you.

You didn't hold me close,
yet I bloomed—
soft and open,
like a flower
greeting spring.

You didn't kiss my forehead,
yet I closed myself gently,
like a lotus
folding into dusk.

You didn't sleep on my lap,
yet my heart
sang a lullaby
just for you.

We didn't search
for each other
in the depths of our eyes,

but you embraced me—
and slipped away
like a song.

As usual.

The Tree That Grew Away From You

It was at dusk
that I plucked myself
from you—
and planted
my trembling heart
in the breast
of wet soil.

In time,
I grew roots.
Sprouted leaves.
Opened my eyes
to a world
I didn't yet know.

Spring brushed me
with its colors.
Autumn sighed
through me.
And winter
passed with a smile,
soft and cold.

I stayed silent—
as if lost
in a long,
unending dream.

When strangers passed,
I opened my umbrella
of branches,
sheltering them
from rain
and sorrow.
Without their knowing,
I took their pain
and offered warmth,
offered love.

Still,
I searched for you
in the songs
of birds
who nested
on my limbs.

I heard your breath
in the breeze
that sometimes
touched me
so gently.

The kisses
once buried
in my roots
rose again—
memories
blossoming
as red flowers
in the quiet of my branches.

They made me beautiful—
a tree full of grace
and green—
while hiding
the ache
of helplessness within.

Even the falling snow
wrote your name
on my leaves.
I bowed my head,
shy
and full of longing.

And one night,
the hands of darkness
gathered me
in their arms
and threw me away
with a passing storm.

Now I ask—
with every trembling leaf:
why did I ever
pluck myself
from you,
only to plant myself
so far away
in this lonely soil?

To the Death

You sit
at a distance,
a contemptuous smile
playing
on your lips.

I stand alone
on this street,
already soaked
in the bitter waters
of failure.

Still,
I wait for you—
to come for me,
to take me
away.

The flowers of hope
fall
petal by petal,
every passing moment
a quiet
undoing.

Will you come
and sit beside me?
Will you carry
my losses
as your own?

Will you gather
my forgotten dreams
and weave them
into your tapestry,
bright
and final?

What is left here
for me
to say goodbye to?

These relationships—
tight knots
of bondage—
lifeless,
like words
stripped of meaning.

The ocean of love
I once carried
has long since
dried.

Friendships,
once cherished,
lie
like half-eaten pages
of dusty books
no one will read again.

Even the veena
I thought I'd carry
into silence
holds only
the pearls of sorrow
strung
by separation.

No one waits
on the steps.
No voice
calls me back.

No hands
reach out
to stop
my journey
with you.

And once we pass
through that door—
the world behind
will begin
to fade.

Dreams,
broken.
Moments,
wet with tears.
Sceneries,
blurred
by the weight of pain.

A little honey,
a little light—
and then,
the long hush
of this death-night.

So when we go,
please—
seal my memories
gently
beneath your
final
blanket.

On the Top of the Hill

At the top of the hill,
Bapu climbed the final step,
paused,
wiped the sweat from his brow,
and turned to look behind.

Shadows moved quietly along the slope—
some advancing, some fading.
In the light of his inner eye,
he saw the fallen faces—
those who could not finish the climb.

At the summit,
Christ and Mohammed welcomed him.
Their conversation was gentle, deep—
a language beyond words.

Buddha spoke softly:
"Welcome to the one
who reached the summit of universal love,

ascending on the path of sacrifice,
with dharma as his walking stick."

Mohammed embraced Gandhi warmly.
Christ held his hands,
his eyes brimming with the kindness
of a thousand forgiven sins.
And in that eternal embrace,
Gandhi became one among them.

As their quiet dialogue bloomed in the air,
others below struggled up the hill—
many tangled in the ropes of bondage,
many burned their feet on the fires of desire.
Some slipped into the pits of pride,
tripped over lies,
and never rose again.

While Christ, Mohammed, and Gandhi
spoke of love and truth above,
down below
men killed each other
in their names.

Some spilled blood to prove
the supremacy of their creed.
And the papers that bore Gandhi's face

turned their backs
on truth and justice.

While the hilltop whispered wisdom,
the steps bled stories,
and the valley below drowned in noise.
Still, the wheel of time rolled forward,
silent,
watching
everything.

Humans

Humans—
how easily
they cast us
into the cages
of forgetfulness,
locking the door
without turning back.

How effortlessly
they trespass
upon the fragile borders
of another's
mental peace—
as if minds
were their playgrounds
to conquer
and abandon.

How quietly,
they dissect the heart—
not with knives,
but with silence.
A silence
sharper
than any weapon.

How easily
they rule
their own little worlds,
never pausing
to weigh the tears,
the aching burdens
carried
by someone else.

Humans.
Humans.
Humans.

So loud
in their triumph.
So quiet
in their cruelty.

How can I write about you?

How can I begin
to write about you?

Your hand—
reaching out
from the folds of a newspaper—
wraps around my neck,
a silent scream
with bones bare of flesh,
eyes buried deep
in hollow sockets
where no blood dares to live.

That fragile hand
leans into me,
and I cannot breathe.

While your parched tongue
pleads for a drop of water,
I am washing my sins
in Coca-Cola—
bought with the price
of rivers I sold.

While your soul
aches with hunger,
my waste
towers sky-high,
a monument
to indifference.

When I am singing about love
sitting in this air-conditioned cabin,
at a distance,
an eagle circles overhead—
waiting for your last breath.

Not only my dreams—
even my death
is bathed in color.
My pride hums softly,
as if untouched.

But what is the color
of your dreams?

Is it
the pale gray of porridge
in a rusted bowl?
The transparent hope
of clean water?
Or the colorless silence
of a tear
too proud to fall?

Now I know—

your lean, trembling hand
holds more strength
than I ever imagined.

It can strangle
not just my comfort,
not just my guilt,
but the whole world
that let you suffer.

If not today,
then one day—
it will.

Come and Sit Beside Me Sometime

Come and sit beside me sometime...

The lanterns of hope
are lighting up—
all at once.

May I fly toward
your boundless kindness?
Toward your priceless presence?
Toward the shelter
of your gentle hands?

May I once again
be the stars
reflected in your eyes?
May I be your gulmohar,
reborn
from a leafless,
branchless death?

The moon smiles at me,
winking quietly.
The breeze pats my shoulder
with its soft hand.
A song travels through the wind
and rests against my heart.
In the distance,
clouds whisper their secrets to me.

Come,
sit beside me sometime,
and tell me—
you loved me
as deeply
as I loved you.

Tell me—
you knew me
as truly
as I knew you.

Tell me—
you cried
thinking of me,
just as I cried
for you.

Tell me—
you missed me
with the ache
I carried
all this time.

Come,
sit beside me sometime.

Though wounds lie hidden in us—
even as we try to know one another—
there are moments
that burned us in the past
but will not burn us again.

Let me give you
my love—
as pure
as clear, flowing water.

Let me offer it to you
in this dusk
that rains blessings
upon us.

How Beautiful Is Death

How beautiful
is death—
in its strange,
unforgiving grace.

How swiftly
it unites us.

Those who
just yesterday
raised weapons
against one another
now join hands—
trembling,
against
a virus
too small to see,
yet vast enough
to humble
humanity.

Religion—
once worn like armor—
is cast into the streets,
no longer
a dividing wall.

It does not matter now.

When death wraps
its cold arms
around a loved one,
suddenly,
humanity
means more
than any god
we shaped in our image.

And the gods?
They sit quietly now,
deep in meditation
in the corners
of abandoned temples,
undisturbed
at last.

How beautiful
is death—
not for what it takes,
but for the truth
it reveals:

that we were always
meant to stand
together.

Thousand Lifetimes of Silence

I am carrying
the pain
of a thousand lifetimes.

I can feel myself
dissolving—
slowly—
into the weight
of this sorrow.

Silent roars
echo within,
filling my eyes
with shadows,
drowning
my soul
in silence.

You see my tears.
You know
I am melting
into this grief—
still,
your hands
do not move.
Still,
your tongue
remains sealed.

And maybe,
just maybe—
this is how
life unfolds
for us all.

Dreams, Fire and Fragility

Born again in your Eyes

You came to me from a faraway place
when my feet were weary
and I had, in spirit, died.

Then—
on the third day—
I rose.

The nails once lodged in my head and heart
fell away
with the gentleness of your touch.

The shroud that death had wrapped around me
turned to a bed of blossoms
beneath your kind embrace.

You lit a lamp
in the darkness of my eyes,
and your song
began to echo
through the silence of my deaf ears.

The 'me' once bound by death
became 'we.'

And in your eyes,
I saw the 'we'—
the eternal,
without birth,
without end.

Where the Stars Still Know Your Name

Friendship
is a shadow
that shelters—
quiet,
constant,
unafraid of the storm.

You can treasure it
even more
than the love
that once wounded
your heart.

Love—
it is a disobedient river.
Even when it knows
it cannot return,
still it flows,

endlessly,
toward the sea.

I have never made
a choice
more painful
than choosing a life
without you—

even knowing
I could not
truly live
without you.

Maybe that is why
some part of me
still belongs to you.
Even after
fate pulled us apart.

Maybe that is why
in the darkness,
you still send me
your light—
reborn
as tiny stars,
scattered across
my sky.

The Many Kinds of Humans

How many kinds of humans walk on this earth!

There are those
who chase colorless dreams,
dipping their hopes
into the fire—
waiting for light to stain
their empty skies.

There are those
who climb high—
faces to the wind,
hearts full of grit—
and glance back
only to marvel
at the thorns they survived.

Some fall—
shattered,
just when they thought
they had it all,
struck down
by life's cruel, sudden turn.

There are quiet ones,
who find joy
in the smallest green—
a new leaf
on a beloved plant,
a soft unfolding of time.

There are the certain ones,
who know nothing—
but live in peace,
thinking they know everything.

Some hide their pain
like sacred fire—
and smile,
as if they carry
sunlight in their bones.

And there are those
who smile
not in warmth,
but in contempt—
spreading shadows
even in the light.

How many kinds of humans walk on this earth!

Where Words Hide

I have so much to write,
until my sorrow finally ends—
but the words
are hiding somewhere,
silent in the shadows.

I want to cry
until my tears turn to ice,
but my eyes are dry,
searching for water
to quench their thirst.

I want to speak
of the journey I began
long ago—
of how I fell to earth
with clipped wings.

Of butterflies
that waited for me,
kissed me gently on my way…

Of the breeze
that pretended to embrace me,
then vanished without a trace.

Of love
that once held my hand so tightly,
only to vanish
like sudden lightning.

Of friendships
I held close—
yet drifted away
without even a word.

Of hope
that fades
with the falling day,

Of dreams
I clutched close to my heart,
yet could not find space
within it.

Of words
trapped in my throat
when I needed them most.

Of life—
that flickers out
like a lamp
with no oil left to burn.

I have so much to write,
until my sorrow finally ends—
but the words
are hiding somewhere,
silent in the shadows.

You Are So Kind

You are so kind.
You gave me time
to heal the wounds
that time had carved into my mind.

You waited patiently beside me,
gently applying
the medicine of your friendship
to every scar.

You are so kind.
The moment I stood close—
close enough to become
the rhythm of your heart—
you welcomed me.

You are so kind.
You embraced me,
if only for a moment,
with your long, slender hands
that held more comfort than words could say.

You are so kind.
You looked with wonder
at the branches of my love,
blossoming—
spreading their quiet fragrance
in your presence.

Once,
you told me
I wasn't in your dreams.

And I said,
you are the only one
who still remains
in mine.

You are so kind.
Still,
you touch my heart
with your warmth—
and with your beauty.

Where my heart ascends...

Oh, my love—
when your voice brushes my ears,
my heart melts like the last snow
on a mountaintop touched by spring.

What can I offer you now
but the silence of this long wait,
this hollow ache
that hums your name in every breath?

What can I sing
but the broken tune
of an old love song,
fragile as a whisper
tossed by the wind?

You are the blessing
I gathered through lifetimes of prayer.

And I—
I am the sunlight
etched into your smile,
a reflection of your warmth.

When night sheds her velvet petals,
and tiny flowers blink open their sleepy eyes,
when your flute meets the breeze
and turns it to music—
a swirl of butterflies
descends upon me.

I rise,
a trembling wing,
a flutter of light—
carried upward
into the heavens
by the echo
of your song.

In Love

Your love—
and your quiet consideration.

The way I know you,
as deeply
as I know myself.

Your silence,
your love—
and the rivers
we flow through
together.

Your desire,
your despair—
and the time
we defeated
side by side.

Your song,
your beautiful eyes—
and the shore
where we once
anchored our souls.

Your love,
and the flowers
you gave me—
and the dusk
when we forgot
each other.

Your dreams,
your moments of sorrow—
and the breeze
that gently wraps
around us both.

My love.
My fortune. Tell me—
who in this world
could ever
separate us?

If You were Rain

If only you were rain—
falling gently on my parched and silent life,
I would have woven a garland
from the tender pearls of your drops.

When the scent of your first touch
rose from the thirst of the earth,
my soul would breathe again—
and I would dissolve into you,
hiding my life within the folds of your rhythm.

If you were rain,
I would let my sorrows melt
into the lullaby of your falling,
each drop a note that sings me into forgetting.

And if you were a song—
I would shed the weight

of all my yesterdays and todays,
and become soil,
soft and surrendering,
receiving you completely.

Bipolar

Your name was Love.
Your eyes—two still lakes
where peace once swam.
Your words flowed
like an ocean of compassion,
your dreams stretched endlessly
beneath the sky.
Your poetry—
a river moving gently through silence.

But you bore another name—Vengeance.
When you poured poison without warning,
my wings turned to ash.
I buried my dreams
in a quiet corner of my heart,
each one drowned
in the venom of your words.

Those who suffered your storm
cursed you without mercy.
Even the mother bird,

who once built her nest upon your branches,
cried out—
her wail lost in the winds
of your rage.

Your love,
your tenderness,
your fury,
your verses,
your cruelty—
And you
were swept away
in the storm
that Time finally summoned.

The Final Wait

I sit on the steps
where dreams once resided,
waiting for you—
though I know
you will not come.

The stars that shimmered
when our eyes first met
once lit my soul
with their quiet fire.

Did you ever know—
when your hand touched mine,
a spark flowed
from skin to soul,
into the earth
beneath our feet?

Did you hear
what the raindrops whispered
as they laughed in my ear
while I sat
so close to you?

Did you ever wish,
as I did,
to vanish from the crowd
and live in a world
where only we existed?

I know—
you will not return.
Still,
I wait
on these steps
where dreams once lived.

I know—
you are bound
by chains of responsibility,
too tired
to break free.

And yet,
I wait.
On these steps.
Still waiting
for you.